Green Pastures

Poems From

Our Westward Move

Martha Rau

Illustrated by Noelle Rau

ISBN: 9798848518870
Imprint: Independently published

For my husband, Lynn,

on the year of our 25th Wedding Anniversary.

Thank you for loving me through

all of our adventures.

Table of Contents

Fall 2020

The Decision

The world has fundamentally changed. On some deep level we're afraid of each another now in a way that we've never been before. We are afraid to speak at the risk of offending this group or that group and starting a riot. Thanks to the Covid pandemic, we are also afraid to talk to each other face to face, sit near one another in the same room, or shake hands. Even within our owns families, we have grown hesitant of touching and hugging.

So, our three teenage daughters, who are somewhat aloof in the best of times, have become even more isolated, skittish and distant; retreating into the virtual world. A virtual world where we have trouble following, let alone, understanding. We can hardly relate to them at all as our own teenage years were so vastly different. Even school has become virtual. Now teenagers might go a full day barely leaving their bedrooms.

On the other hand, as adults, we long for wide open spaces. We shun crowded rooms, drive past abandoned theaters, eat at home, and skip the Fair. Naturally, we worry about the impact of all this virtual living on our children's physical and mental health.

So, in the light of these changes and concerns, my husband, Lynn and I have made the difficult decision to move from our home of thirteen years in the suburbs of southern Maryland to rural South Dakota. We plan to buy land from my husband's aunt and uncle. We hope to build a house, a shop, a barn, have a big garden, a horse, and raise a few chickens. We hope to give our daughters experiences we remember from places we loved growing up. We wish to remind them that a beautiful real world still exists beyond the confines of their electronic devices.

I have been waiting for a sign from God that moving is the right thing to do, but I think my husband got the sign. He has the burning in his heart to return to the place he knew as a boy and reconnect with his family. I certainly cannot begrudge him that. Besides, I have always loved horses.

Fear not for I am with you; I will bring your offspring from the east, and from the west I will gather you.

Isaiah 43:5

The Crooked Star

December 2020

The star looks crooked
on our hallway Christmas tree.
I tried in vain to fix it
for expectant joy to see.

But it drooped again to one side
like a tired waning light.
And I reached out across the stair rail
in an attempt to make it right.

It perked up for an instant
and stood up tall and straight.
I said now that is perfect
our Christmas will be great.

Then, in the next instant
it tilted far over to one side.
And I thought, this atrocity
I just cannot abide!

But last night I began to ponder
on that star's off-kilter veering.
How appropriate for this year
with all its sideways steering.

These blurred months seem so strange
and now we hear Christmas tunes.
With no chance of seeing distant family
to lift our separate lonely glooms.

No more eager joy of children
wishing for Christmas morn
Just a lot of packing boxes
and a front door wreath forlorn.

I thought it could be relaxing
a quiet Christmas in this house.

But I find preparations taxing
with my somber teens and spouse.

I hoped that putting up the trees
would pump joy to my heart.
Instead, I just feel stretched
like worn stitches torn apart.

Mary on that first Christmas
must have felt a little frayed
by the time she and Joseph
got to the stable where they stayed.

She probably would have enjoyed a bath
and a pillow for her head.
Some ice chips for her throat
and a supportive birthing bed.

But she managed with God's help
in less-than-ideal conditions.
And that is a poignant lesson
when I'm fretting foiled traditions.

Not all Christmases are perfect
and sometimes hope seems very far.
But holy light glows just as brightly
through a blessed and crooked star.

*And she gave birth to her first-born son and wrapped him
in swaddling clothes and laid him in manger because there
was no place for them in the inn.*

Luke 2:7

2021

The Long Good-bye

After the initial tear-filled explosion of telling your children,
preparing to move cross-country is like pulling a Band-Aid off
slowly so that it rips each individual hair from your arm.
I almost wish to remove it all at once
rather than endure again the bittersweet agony of
the Long Good-bye.

Instead, we begin by working at the sticky edges.
Painting a room
donating some unused items
packing up a box here and there
telling a few close friends.
All pretty innocuous.
You can almost fool yourself into believing it is happening to
someone else.

Then, the first load of tools and garage items
heads west in a yellow Penske truck and
you start to realize, "this is happening to *me.*"

But at that same time, the "new normal" continues
virtual school, writing, laundry, husband working from home,
online shopping
the occasional masked foray to the store.

Next, awareness of 'the lasts' begins:
The last Thanksgiving here
the last time I'll put up Christmas decorations in this house
the last time the twins have their friends since Kindergarten to
celebrate their birthday here.

And in a year where normal traditions are suspended you realize that
the last of many things already happened.
You were unaware, so you failed to savor the moment
Now you can't quite remember exactly what transpired that day.
The last time singing with the choir,
the last time teaching Sunday School,
the last in-person Bible study,

the last time in church on Sunday,
the last soccer game for the girls
the last day of in-person school with their friends and
teachers.

Saying no to long term commitments begins
Savoring snatched time with friends on walks
and at the park
final dentist and doctor appointments.

There is a gradual pulling away
and distancing yourself,
knowing your investment in the current place
has become short-term.

Then, begins serious packing of boxes
full-house painting and deep cleaning,
meeting with real estate agents,
and the house stager.

Friends bring food because you
have manic-sad-stress eyes and
your voice cracks when you talk on the phone.

You remember with sinking heart how the Long Good-bye
felt before in Delaware, Florida, Georgia, and Texas.

You attempt to maintain an attitude of hope about the future
during an extended period of contagious uncertainty
while your daughters continually bombard you with doubts,
fears, and searing remarks
that loop on continuous play in your head.

The house sells.

You savor how the light floods favorite rooms
at different times of the day
Memorize trees and plantings
A pain knots in your chest like a part of you is dying.
Final embraces.

Feeling a kinship with the pioneers.

And when the Band-Aid is finally off
you note the sticky residue.
And how the wound has not yet healed.

But some part of you acknowledges
with deep and abiding thankfulness
that you made wonderful friends
and dwelt in a lovely home
where children grew from high chair to High School.

I am grateful for a place so worthy of
the Long Goodbye.

We know that in everything God works for good with those who love him, who are called according to his purpose.

Romans 8:28

An Earlier Journey to Bethlehem

God clicks the puzzle pieces into place.
He sets the stage for grand events before.
Watch him connect people through holy grace
and draw direct lines we cannot ignore.

Before the famous journey to enroll
young virgin, Mary and husband brave.
The one with shepherds on a starry knoll.
Angels singing of baby come to save.

Two fragile widows trod a dessert road
Naomi bereft of husband and of sons
heads back to Judah with a heavy load
knowing past days of joy have been undone.

Wanting to return where she belonged
But Ruth would not let her journey alone
She clung to her with heart so pure and strong
and in her faithful choices brightly shone.

Boaz saw in poor gleaning Ruth the light
and took her for his wife and Jesse's root.
Giving to Mara, Naomi's delight.
A son, Obed from loyal daughter, Ruth.

From the lineage of Jesus Christ in Mathew:

And Salmon the father of Boaz by Rahab, and Obed the father of Jesse, and Jesse the father of David the king.

Matthew 1:5-6

Journey and Trip

Journey and Trip Lifeman were full brothers.
Same dark graying hair and tall lanky height.
Afar, you could not tell one from the other
Warm dimpled smiles and brown eyes so bright.
Scuffed travel bags with straps of wide leather
Plain oxford shoes, never quite tied just right.
The same jacket for nights of cool weather.

Yet between, lay the gap of an ocean.
Trip went places to check his to-do lists.
While traveling, he chose constant motion.
Whether for work, play, or eyeing vistas
he aimed to complete a pre-set notion.
He knew where he would rest his head each night.
Set his alarm, and in morning, he rose.
He never had time for off-road delights.
Followed agenda with neat and fresh clothes.
Trip knew the exact date he would come home,
knew the time he'd arrive and prop his feet,
knew the tv scheduled game in the dome
and what meal he would microwave to eat.
He might be alone, his house so quiet
occasional questions circling his mind.
But no one annoyed or forced him to diet.
He thought religion seemed meant just to bind.
so pushed thoughts aside that caused him to doubt.
And pulled down the shades to keep the sun out.

Journey's travels were much diff'rent than Trip's
With thoughtful gaze and beginnings of beard,
he cared not for time's harsh calendar flips.
Listening in prayer for plans where to veer,
he discovered sites along narrow paths,
wrote in his journal with tall looping strokes,
sketched in the margins, remembered to laugh.
He slept when he wearied and spoke with new folks.
never seemed rushed or hassled or frantic.

Wore out his soles and learned much about life.
Even made time for picnics romantic.
He wept o'er darkness and cities in strife
and leapt at the chance to marry his wife.
At dawn he praised sunrises over the bay.
Looked west when the sun glowed with bright fire,
marveled and struggled for right words to say.

Later, down a lane lined with blooms to admire
Journey sat down by a vine-covered gate.
He took off his shoes and rubbed his sore feet.
He waited for Trip, as the hour grew late
in hopes that his brother, soon he would meet.

The spot was peaceful with shade from high clouds
Then, just as his eyelids began to close,
he heard distant trumpets blowing quite loud.
Startled and barefoot, he quicky arose.
The gate swung open with nary a creak,
shown brilliance within too wondrous to speak.

Trust in the Lord with all your heart, and do not rely on your own insight. In all your ways acknowledge him and he will make straight your paths.

Proverbs 3:5-6

The Beast of Homesickness

Homesick grief is a sneaky, loathsome beast
who emerges at close of busy days.
Puffs up like gooey dough with too much yeast
to ooze past edges and strike poison flays.

Spews harsh words in vile looping hate.
Lava melting tender shoots of hope
while molten salty tears drench untouched plates.
Threatening no slim chance to ever dare cope.

If all loved friends and familiar joys live east
where we rested on bright earned reputes,
what point to try here in the unknown west
and make great effort like fresh new recruits?

The beast roars, "New equals disloyalty!"
All tiny sprigs of green amid the snow
must be squashed with old school fealty
or risk a thaw of anger's icy hold.

The beast feeds on past memories and fear.
He misses sunsets of magenta hue
by circling always to thoughts far from here.
He distracts from folks who long to know you.

He fails to see the prairie's grand spaces
and yearns for the deep coastal waterways.
He shuns the mighty Missouri traces
and moans for lost opportunity days.

But what he fears more than all change and new
is how time dulls the sharpest pangs of grief
unlocks the gate for hope's flood true
and as months go by brings unsought relief.

The Lord is near to the brokenhearted,
and saves the crushed in spirit.

Psalm 34:18

Mexican Strawberries

March 31ˢᵗ 2021

Strange how the world has gotten smaller
and bigger at the same time.
If you told me last March that I would
be eating strawberries grown in Mexico
at my kitchen table
in a little house in Selby, South Dakota
1500 miles away,
I would not have believed you.
I would have laughed like Sarah when she learned she would
bear a child in her old age.
In hindsight it all makes sense.
Well, not *perfect* sense,
but if you lay out all the facts
you can see the reasoning.

As I was writing this, a friend back in Maryland
sent picture of a strawberry she had for lunch.
It had the top cut off and was facing the camera
showing a heart shape inside.

God's love is inside everything.

We love because God first loved us.

1 John 4:19

The Little House in Town

The house is unassuming.
Change the radio station and you've missed it.
White with peeling blue-gray trim
Wedged between a drive-in restaurant and a trucking company
Dwarfed by a giant evergreen
heavy with birds.

Parts of the house are a hundred years-old
That's how old I felt when we arrived.
Worn down and slightly shabby
with sketchy plumbing.

But, there are treasures to be found
cut glass doorknobs on antique wood doors
ample storage, a cozy heater
Best of all, it was available when we needed it.
Being available gets a bad rap.

I hope when I get to the Pearly Gates,
St. Peter glances at his clipboard and
says to one of the angels,
"Let her in. She wasn't always the best
but she was available when He called."

So what if the neighbors want
the house torn down.
It has a roomy porch.
and I think we'll rest awhile in its shade.

Who knows.
Perhaps, with a touch of paint and some
flowers we can turn an available house
into a beloved home.

Then I said, "Here am I! Send me."

Isaiah 6:8b

Gypsy

Gypsy, the wandering Quarter Horse mare
Born near the river on Five Arrow farm
with gentle brown eyes and thick raven hair
Endowed with wild spirit, beauty and charm.

On Christmas Day of year forty-seven
I unwrapped a photo beneath our tree.
The news all around so unlike Heaven
but the photo awoke a dream in me.

My love with pandemic beard-hidden grin
and a mare without stable, pasture or rope.
A horse before moving or building begins.
Never a gift of purer faith and hope.

Fast forward some tough months of house selling,
Leaving the sunrises over the Bay
Feverish packing, farewells, and traveling
to maraschino skies o'er plains faraway.

Here lives the wandering Quarter Horse mare
with gentle brown eyes and thick raven hair.
Born near the river on Five Arrow Farm
Endowed with wild spirit, beauty, and charm.

Really quite regal and boss of the pen.
Some days I ride and feel almost girlish.
until she bucks me and stomps at the men.
I leave feeling rumpled, dusty, and foolish.

At fourteen hands two with smooth liquid gaits
her root beer coat glows with glazed amber sheen.
Her lineage and breeding clearly first rate.
To me she is lovelier than any queen.

Snowy anklets round each dainty rear hoof.
She measures me up; finds my skills lacking.
She acts towards me a little aloof.
Perhaps it's my style or rusty tacking.

Perhaps she misses her Chicago days.
I'm not an expert, nor deign to pretend
But I will persist with calm patience praise.
Treat her with love 'til we come to the end.

Hopefully, one day 'ere sunflowers bloom
she'll hear my call and think more than carrots.
And I'll know that her heart finally made room
though she might never wish to declare it.

Gypsy, the wandering Quarter Horse mare
Born near the river on Five Arrow farm
with gentle brown eyes and thick raven hair.
Endowed with wild spirit, beauty and charm.

Shire

Fuzzy foggy stripes ablur
A baby's cry and motorboat purr
Streaking past my kitchen seat
fluid movements, soundless feet

Climbing up the carpet wall
getting stuck, a plaintive call
Ignoring rules and chewing cords
Sharpened claws like miniature swords

Teasing canine, surprise attacks
Tail puffed out and ears flat back
Sits on paws without any fears
Submits to bathing of his ears

Slinking through the darkened basement
Perching in our window casements
Watching birds with feral eyes
A hunter's gaze in playful guise

Pharaoh sprawled out on a bed
Dark eyelines and regal head
Worn out from his sideways running
Coat all warm from midday sunning

Limp joints like a soggy noodle
Heart as sweet as sugary strudel
Tender cuddles, drying tears
Easing stress and calming fears

A lazy silky acrobat
is my eldest daughter's cat.

Drought Sonnet

Violent wind whips dust across parched fields
of prairie grass burnt yellow to the roots.
Thirsty yards crunch 'neath silty cowboy boots
crushing spring hopes of green abundant yields.

I too, wilt wordlessly behind faith's shield
while scorching sun destroys young fragile shoots.
Await a shower of inspiring fruits
and pray liquid mercies be revealed.

You Lord, could so easily send some rain
To coax my limp and lifeless blooms to burst,
To cleanse our dirty opaque window panes,
and quench the cracked ground's deep gnawing thirst.

Until then, I seek wisdom yet again
to know that we are loved, not cursed.

***Then he (Elijah) prayed again and the heaven gave rain,
and the earth brought forth its fruit.***

James 5:18

Touring Lake Oahe

Touring Lake Oahe on a friends' pontoon
we passed a car stuck in the river sand.
Marooned on vacant stretch of fishing shore
with no one near to lend a helpful hand.

We shook our heads over their dilemma
but continued with our languid snoozing
Surely someone else would stop to aid them.
Then I forgot, and enjoyed our cruising.

Distracted by azure Missouri depths,
sundrenched warmth and clear cerulean skies,
plains dipping down to drought exposed beaches
Blush of sunburn creeping up bare thighs

Such a much-needed peaceful afternoon.
But my love remembered those sunken tires
and felt a burning of a different kind.
An insistent nudging about the mire.

So, when the boat was stowed and farewells said
we returned to beach and the sound of thanks
as he aided them to free their car
Using skills he learned from the Outer Banks.

Now, my husband is a bit skeptical
So, he might well another version share.
And yet, I perceived the Holy Spirit
blowing through him, though he was unaware.

*The wind blows where it wills, and you hear the sound of it,
but you do not know whence it comes or whither it goes;
so it is with everyone who is born of the spirit.*

John 3:8

Grateful for Rain

Thank you, Lord for sending rain
to tap upon my bedroom pane.
Coaxing tomato vines to grow
and washing dust from car windows.
Soaking fields and quenching thirsty ground.
Soothing fears with gentle thrumming sound.
Unfurling withered leaves like flags.
Making evergreen boughs to sag
with weight of water sweet and rare.
Crystal drops of answered prayers.

Amen

Let us fear the Lord our God, who gives the rain in its season, the autumn rain, and the spring rain, and keeps for us the weeks appointed for the harvest.

Jeremiah 5:24

Mustard Seeds

What is zeal?
Who has fervor anymore?
I listlessly toss out mustard seeds
with dwindling hope shorn up
by stubborn principle.

Wishing one might morph into a seedling
or a scraggly bush.
But not daring to believe that miracle
will actually come to pass.
Always bracing for the next disappointment.
Preparing for rejection.

Maybe that's the problem.
I am too short-sighted.
Limiting my view of God to a grain
because I cannot imagine the breadth of the mustard tree
or feeling the wind in my hair as I swing from its branches
or watching the birds dwell in its shade.

But while there is the slimmest chance
some version might take root and flourish
into a stalwart tree,
I will keep planting seeds and waiting.

Because isn't that what He means?
Even miniscule bits of faith can move mountains.

For truly I say to you, if you have faith as a grain of
mustard seed, you will say to this mountain, 'Move from
here to there,' and it will move; And nothing will be
impossible to you."

Mathew 17:20

A Time to Eat Peaches

Peaches are time sensitive
I've tasted enough bad ones to know.
Sunset orbs mounded in the produce section
tempt me with delights of summers' past.

At home, they beckon from the fruit bowl
like a glossy magazine photo.
Too eager, I snatch one.
The peel clings persistently,
taunting the knife.

The hard-won sections disappoint
with flavorless cardboard crunches
unaided by sprinkles of sugar
and corn syrupy cereal.

Or, patience turns to forgetfulness and
too many mornings pass
until the peach bounces wrinkled and rubbery
into the garbage pail.

Others are simply bruised
or mealy from the beginning;
evading ripening into anything useful
or marginally edible.

But once in a great while
I gently squeeze one feeling
the perfect hopeful squish.
The peel practically falls off
A solid pit pops from an inside
dripping with golden sweetness.
The perfect peach.

It leaves me craving more peaches;
Yellow peaches, white peaches,
Georgia peaches, Washington peaches,

peaches on breakfast cereal,
peach salsa and peach cobbler,

Thank you, God for delicious ripe peaches
the vast variety of fruits
and the miracles of modern transit.

I do not begrudge the unripe
or rotten peaches along the way.
Forgotten are the long peach-less months
amidst the glory of a distant tree's success.
Oh, to be fruitful like that peach tree.

Perhaps, we cling too much to the idea
of being continuously fruitful
In comparing ourselves to others
seemingly more bountiful.

We forget God created unique fruits
and different seasons for a reason.
Without the seasons of failures,
disappointments and frozen fruits,
we would not so celebrate
a time to eat peaches.

*For everything there is a season and a time for every matter
under heaven; a time to be born and a time to die;
a time to plant and a time to pluck up what is planted.*

Ecclesiastes 3:1-2

Blackberries

My sister is a treasure hunter
who wades through fields of thorns.
She seeks neither gold, nor diamonds
nor poaches rhino horns.

She journeys not through distant lands
or dives beneath dark seas.
Instead, she pulls on rubber boots
with pants tucked round her knees.

With plastic bowl in hand
ventures forth to comb the brambles
Floppy brim to shade her eyes
on her sultry July rambles.

Steady and persistent
though her arms crisscross with scratches.
Locates the onyx clusters
in their secret woodland patches.

Gently raises prickly branches
dripping jewels from slender limbs.
Ah, the elusive wild blackberry!
She could sing a joyful hymn.

Imagining the purply jelly jars
fills her bowl with trembling fingers.
Musing over berry cobbler
while the smell of sweetness lingers.

Berry remnants to dye homespun.
No ounce of gemstone wasted.
Always grateful for her prizes.
A successful quest well-tasted.

So, dear friend, remember
when your life seems all in shambles
Sometimes priceless fruits emerge
through enduring thorny brambles.

More than that, we rejoice in our sufferings, knowing that suffering produces endurance; and endurance produces character; and character produces hope.

Romans 5:3-4

Zucchini

A gargantuan zucchini plant
the likes of which I'd never hosted in a garden before.
A proud forest of sticky prickly stalks
supporting leaves the size of baby elephant ears.

Flopping over the side of the raised bed,
they overshadowed the youthful string beans and
entombed infant zucchini nubs in darkness.
Separated from the sun, with no room to grow
they were stunted and rotting.

Pruning
It pained me, but I did it.
With untrained fingers,
trimmed the stalks all around the bottom to
let the breeze and sunlight in,
giving the youngsters space to expand
into the fullness of stir fry and zucchini bread.

Pruning
Vital to fruitfulness.
Yet it's hard to cut off green leaves during a drought
when the land is parched and barren around us.
It seems wrong, counterintuitive.
I am grateful for anything is growing.

But up close, some of the leaves had brown spots.
They were not as beautiful as they seemed from afar.
And, if we allow too many thirsty leaves
no energy or space remains for good fruit.

Every branch of mine that bears no fruit,
he takes away, and every branch that does bear fruit,
he prunes, that it may bear more fruit.

John 15:2

Islands on the Prairie

Back east one town flows into another seamlessly.
A blur of houses, stores, and businesses merged together
in an unending strip of activity.
Only the post office knows
where one town ends and another begins.

Here, each town is an island floating
on a sea of prairie grass speckled with cattle.
Linked to its fellows by rolling highways
or unmarked gravel byways.

After miles of grass, grainfields and sunflowers,
from a great distance rising above the plains,
one sees the enormous silver grain bins and elevators
towering over the landscape like giant tin men.

Entering town is an event complete with
truck braking, welcome signage,
local billboards ads,
and high school championship history.

A water tower, a gas station store combo,
a bar restaurant and bait shop,
a hardware store, houses, churches, and a cuff of trees
encircling the group to stave off the fiercest wind.

Each town shows a unique personality and island flavor.
pride in its own, the sense of multi-generational identity,
a comforting connection to place
and even its own weather.

Birds

God presses on some hearts
to feed the birds.
To fill mismatched feeders beneath the evergreen tree
while the full moon still hovers overhead
caught in dawn's door.
To observe their raucous feasting
and fluttering from a kitchen window.

He could feed them some other way, certainly.
But He gives us the opportunity
to serve in this small way.
And their spontaneous operas,
scarlet caps, painted feathers,
and the smiling sunflower patch they planted
by our burgundy bird bath
bring me joy.

Look at the birds of the air: they neither sow nor reap nor gather into barns, and yet your heavenly Father feeds them. Are you not of more value than they?

Matthew 6:26

Mama Spider Plant

Our spider plant had a baby!
No need for presents or a card
or tiny baby booties
or toys to play with in the yard.

Just a private water shower
with me and her best friend,,
a droopy spinster cactus,
her loyal companion to the end.

We praise the new addition
with her flowers dainty white
A pompom dangling on a string
Such a fragile green delight

Heir of a kindergarten sprig,
delivered Dixie cup express,
who lived and reigned prolific
from my counter to impress.

One of three plants to move
west with us this year,
she nearly froze to death
in a hotel lot partway here.

Then languished in the laundry room
for months just scraping by.
Until I moved her to the living room
in hopes that she'd revive.

And now on the eve of high school
chubby hands all long and slender.
She sprouts another baby
so this lesson we remember.

Endure change like the spider plant.
God is with you in all places
You can survive the darkness
'til sunshine lights your faces.

Be strong and of good courage; be not frightened, neither be dismayed; for the Lord your God is with you wherever you go.

Joshua 1:9

A Spontaneous Act of Sweetness

My eldest and I are going through a rough patch
More than a patch-
a rough field mined
with those sharp prickly thistles
that hurt your fingers when you pull them out.
She is angry at us.
She is angry at me.
She says cruel hateful words.
She oscillates between anger and despair.
I nag her too much.
I cry too often.

Yet, the other night she kissed me on the cheek
when she got home and I was already in bed.
A spontaneous act of sweetness
that gave me hope.

Love bears all things, believes all things,
hopes all things, endures all things. Love never ends.

I Corinthians 13:7-8

Ode to the Barn

Seeing a barn means
someone had dreams.
They treasured a parcel of land
Hoped and planned for the future
Tilled, planted, and harvested
Cared for animals.

Did I tell you we're building a red barn
on a hill that can be seen for miles?
It is our new beginning
A foothold on the prairie
The first building on our land
A step forward
A home base
A hilltop cathedral
from which to admire sunsets.

August Sunflowers

Loyal Sunflower tracks the golden light
From dawn 'til dusk faces the distant fire
Brown eye fixed to August rays admire
Coyly batting her yellow lashes bright
An ardent lover swaying with delight
Gathering round a bath for wayward birds
or dancing playfully in wind-tossed herds
chanting their harvest chorus with brilliant might.

Why not wake each morn with Sunflower's hope?
Worship God with joyful petals unfurled
Spread seeds and bask within the growing light
Follow in faith each day with focused scope
to illuminate shadows in the world
and witness radiance beyond earth's sight.

***The light shines in the darkness,
and the darkness has not overcome it.***

John 1:5

A Writer's Prayer

Lately I have begun to despair over my work.
Are my stories never to see the light of day?
Are the characters I conjured and nurtured
and danced onto the pages
always to remain entombed on my laptop?
Are the heroes and villains I represent
to stay trapped in their endless looping world
forever beautiful and clever, handsome and valiant
ageless and separate?

I believed you applauded my efforts
and inspired me to give them life.
To arm them with courage, valor and tenacity
to fight their foes?
My heart raced as their adventures flooded the pages.

You could so easily prompt a
a literary gatekeeper to crack the door
and permit my sagas to spill out
into the world of print
to enflame the imaginations
and touch the hearts of readers.

Will you continue to let people believe me fruitless?
That I futilely tap away for years on my husband's dime
creating magical unseen worlds filled with good an evil
and all manner of treachery thwarted by triumphant light
as the novels of others pop up on stands
like leaves unfurling after the rain?

Meanwhile, I scour the internet.
I plead my case before scores of virtual book lords
I even pray for them before pressing send.
Only to be politely rejected or ignored.
I am too embarrassed to even speak
my tales to friends and family anymore.

My heroes rattle the bars of their two-dimensional jail.
Please release them from bondage
to live and battle and love in the sunlight.
Let them no longer be shunned pariahs.

How can I continue to endure their confinement?
How can stand strong against the silent ridicule
of those who think me a foolish middle-age woman
avoiding real employment?

If it is truly your will that I turn in another direction
please enlighten me with a sign
Inspire me with some nugget of wisdom.
Give me an idea tied with a bright ribbon
and wrapped in peace.

Or help me stay this course.
For I walk a tightrope strand of hope,
all that remains of the wide bridge
of breathless excitement
once crossing the deep chasm of failure.

I am assured you have a plan unfolding.
You, who can turn a shepherd into a king
a cupbearer to into a rebuilder of walls
an old woman into mother of a great people
and a runaway prince into leader of captive nation.

Please forgive my frank advocacy
and despairing dreams.
I know there are far greater problems
in the world of today.

But all pride has left me
I am humbled before you
Help me be open to your plans
Supply me with patience and fortitude
and strengthen my slender lifeline of hope
as you did for so many of
the characters in your own Good Book.

Chariots of Fire

Sometimes when God hears our cries
he pulls us out from sinking mire
or whispers gently to the wind
or with sun and rain conspires.

Sometimes He sends a person
to help the situation dire
or points you to the perfect verse
when your heavy burdens tire.

Sometimes there appear no answers
to your heart's deepest desires,
And your pleas go on for years
while your hopes and dreams retire.

I don't expect parted seas
or a voice from bush afire
I don't expect instant cures
or a nation to inspire.

I don't expect to build an ark
or fell Jericho's mighty spires.
I surely believe they happened
and their stories I do admire.

Those just aren't the answers
my myopic prayers require.

So, before the Breeder's Auction
we read 'bout each dam and sire
And I prayed for help choosing
a horse Daughter might desire

Auction night arrived and the
barn was full of veteran buyers
But as the auctioneer sped fast
and the bids climbed ever hirer

I crossed off each favorite colt
on my crumpled auction flyer.
My daughter squeezed my hand
and hope almost did expire

Then, the handsome buckskin filly
with the white upon her face
planted her feet and looked at us
and an anxious bid I placed.

We thought her far beyond our grasp
with pedigree so prestigious
and our chances running out
for best laid plans egregious.

Then, surprise! the bidding stopped
Our number was recorded.
We had a filly for our own
at a price we found afforded.

So, despite my limited faith
(His good humor, I admire)
He provided a horse called,
Five Arrow's Chariots of Fire.

Just remember my dear friends
The Good Book might seem older
But God still sends chariots of fire.
So, make that praying bolder.

*Then Elisha prayed, and said,
'O Lord, I pray thee, open his eyes that he may see,'
so the Lord, opened the eyes of the young man,
and he saw; and behold, the mountain was full of horses
and chariots of fire round about Elisha.*

2 Kings 6:17

Magic Cookies

The cookies magically appeared in the Kitchen,
complete with that delightful fresh-baked cookie smell.
There were no dishes or pans in the sink and
no sticky residue on the marbled Formica countertop.

When I went to work on the barn there were no cookies.
When I came home, sweaty and bedraggled,
Poof! A clear plastic container
filled with chocolate chip cookies
like a delicious mirage.
The only logical explanation, of course,
magic cookies.

Because every middle-aged mom knows that homemade food
does not simply appear in the Kitchen.
Food disappears from the Kitchen
This often happens late at night when the gnomes come out.
Mostly empty to-go boxes appear in the fridge.
partially eaten potato chips bags roll around the counter
dirty, food crusted plates and bowls sneak into the sink,
but rarely, if ever, does made-from-scratch food,
show up on its own with the no explanation.
Definitely, magic cookies.

One of the hardest things about being an adult, and a mom,
besides the lower metabolism and the constant worry,
is coming to terms with the loss of magic.
You know what I mean.
The magic your own mom or grandmom made happen.
All those meals and desserts she made
that miraculously appeared on the table.
What a gift, to have someone prepare food for you.
Like, magic cookies.

Later I discovered, it was my daughter, Noelle
who made those magic cookies on that October day.

Thank you, Noelle, for showing me magic again.

Turning Point

The end of the October and our barn seems
a cruel folly, a thorn, an albatross.

My mind can barely conjure horses
grazing against a backdrop of red.
All I see is rain and mud.
All I feel is the buffeting wind
and the brutal numbness of freezing wet fingers.

My stalwart husband even appears downhearted.
Our helpful outdoorsy daughter, has begun to bow out

Worse, a foul hopeless spirit floats around our little house in town
encouraging despair and bitter nostalgia for our previous situation.

Harsh words
Blame slapped around.
Short tempers.
Normal tasks appearing overwhelming
and the threat of looming winter cultivating urgent desperation.

Laughable, that we even considered by now we would
be living in new house on the prairie
instead of struggling to tin the sides of a barn in the wind.

And yet, there is much to be grateful for.
Our house in town is warm, we have plenty of food.
We are healthy, our extended family is kind and helpful,
I am able to fashion warm hats from balls of thick yarn,
the fuzzy dog loves us,
the cat entertains with his playful shenanigans,
and the Methodists let me sing with them.

Every great story has a turning point
when the heroine flounders and then chooses to press on.
Even Jonah, the reluctant prophet, chose to pray
from the belly of the fish

"...when my soul fainted within me,
I remembered the Lord;
and my prayer came to thy holy temple."
Jonah 2:7

Ask anyone with gray hair
They've all had turning points
Things worth building well take faith,
hard work, and a long while to complete.
Years are but an instant to the Lord.

For every house is built by someone,
but the builder of all things is God.

Hebrews 3:4

Joy and Happiness

Joy and Happiness rode off across the fields together
Two friends, side by side, pleased with sunshine and fair weather.
In appearance quite alike, with jeans and dusty boots.
Same stature, shining steeds, and playful glee-filled hoots.

Happiness roared, "What a glorious day, let's race."
and bolted off at a breakneck pace.
Joy cheered, "Praise the Lord for all He's done!"
and galloped towards the rising sun.

Now, Happiness rode a wild horse, unpredictable and fleeting
One moment, straight and true
the next, he swerved her out of seating.
He bucked, she sailed into the air and landed with a thud.
Moaning and discouraged, she lay there in the mud.

But Joy rode a steady mount
not scared or daunted by bleak weather.
He carried her with grace as they traveled on together.
She marveled at the sunsets, admired the silvery moon
Was grateful for the little things
like when she sang in tune.

Joy squinted to see Happiness as they climbed up steep inclines
and picked their way through rocks or got tangled up in vines.
Sometimes Happiness disappeared for endless days
as Joy soldiered on through shade and dappled rays.

Finally, clouds lifted and Happiness appeared ahead
Rosey cheeked and laughing, with not a single hint of dread.
The two loped on together, side by side, across the prairie
enjoying a bright afternoon with no dark thoughts to carry.

Knowing Happiness was fickle
Joy loved her anyway.
And thanked God for the chance to
ride with her another day.

Though the fig tree do not blossom,
nor fruit be on the vines,
the produce of the olive fail
and the fields yield no food,
the flock be cut off from the fold
and there be no herd in the stalls,
yet I will rejoice in the Lord,
I will joy in the God of my salvation.
God, the Lord, is my strength;
he makes my feet like hinds' feet,
he makes me tread upon my high places."

Habakkuk 3:17-19

A *Mary* Christmas Season

A Martha Christmas schedule
with baking, bows, and singing.
With Christmas trees and parties
and Santa his gifts bringing.

Months of warm handmade items
all in totes for a local show.
Crocheted and knit with care
with a just a few more things to go.

Desiring a family photo
with bright and smiling faces
and gifts all wrapped ahead
to send to far off places.

Wanting to be organized
Christmas cards all in the mail
and festive twinkling lights
dangling from the front porch rail.

Instead, this Advent Season
Here I sit knitting on my bed,
or sleeping through my coughing
with decongestants in my head.

Perhaps I should switch focus
and temper my busy plans.
Listen to Jesus with my heart
and not depend on busy hands.

So, while this wretched virus
has me limp, behind, and beat
Forget about my list and spend
a *Mary* Christmas at His feet.

*…And a woman named Martha received him into her
house. And she had a sister called Mary, who sat at the
Lord's feet and listened to his teaching. But Martha was
distracted with much serving; and she went to him and said,
"Lord, do you not care that my sister has left me to serve
alone? Tell her to help me," But the Lord answered her,
"Martha, Martha, you are anxious and troubled about
many things; one thing is needful. Mary has chosen the
good portion, which shall not be taken away from her."*

Luke 10: 38-42

2022

Forgotten Love

When Love dawned newly shiny
no task was too much trouble.
With its infant feet so sweet and tiny
It made our joy to bubble.

For family, friends and neighbors all
our work served a higher call.
We took pride in mundane tasks and chores
and made delicious plans like Smores

"All for Love" we cried with cheerful hearts.
Let Love bless you with its light.
Come friends and listen to this happy news
Fill the world with music bright."

But then, Love seemed to need constant tending.
As time passed it taxed us more
It required food, warm clothes, shelter, mending
and we missed the younger flame,

One bleak day, we looked around
to see joyous Love once more.
And to our great dismay, instead we found
merely a shadow remained.

Three reigning stewards, strong and mostly good.
In the place of Love now stood
Their names; Habit, Tradition, and Duty.
Sometimes they became tired, bored or snooty.

We mistook them for Love.

I mistook them for Love.

I labored through the busy sunless days
I washed dishes and folded clothes
Missing Love's abundant rays
Forgetting to pat my dog's soft nose.

I shopped and fixed us ample food
I typed many dutiful words
but forgot to feed the hungry birds,
I ignored my daughters' sullen moods.

Failed to ask more about their trials
listen well, or make them smile.
Motored through holidays without much rest
Cringed when people made requests.

I worked hard to forgive some little wrongs
Attempted to forget enough
to keep relations on the surface strong.
So, I could check that task off my list.

Oh, I endured all my chores all right
but I forgot to show delight.
Only grumbled, whined and turned quite hateful.
For my efforts, I thought Love ungrateful.

So that you might not make the same mistake
I confess this with a heart that aches.
I got so busy doing things for Love
That I forgot *who* Love is,

"I know you are enduring patiently and bearing up for my name's sake, and you have not grown weary. But I have this against you, that you have abandoned the love you had at first.

Revelation 2:3-4

A Whiff of Spring
February 7, 2022

This morning I caught a faint whiff of Spring.
Crazy as that sounds with winter all around.
Me, bundled up in my heavy hat and coat
sensing the fresh aroma of growing things awaking.

But it was enough to make me pause, hand on the door.
To hear a fresh note in the in the bird's song
to sense a lightning in the air
easing the weight on my chest

to feel a spark of hope.
Hope enough, perhaps, to open the new seed catalog.
Hope that we've now come further than remains.
More deep winter lays behind us, than ahead.

Like Noah, when the dove brought him the olive leaf.
Deep waters surrounding the ark.
knowing they would not recede for weeks.
But new hope the sea would not reign forever.

Like a horse turning for home during a long ride,
the spring in her step, the straining at the bit,
knowing, sight unseen, the direction of the barn.
Hope of fresh hay, friends, and cool water awaiting.

Like a runner looping back toward home,
the quickening of his heartbeat,
the lengthening of his stride,
his ears strained for cheers of onlookers at the finish line,

I believe we are on the far side of pandemic.
The dense fog is clearing, the water's beginning to recede.
We've come through more than yet remains.
Yes, there are still uncharted depths and storms ahead.

But the grasp of winter darkness is weaking.
The birds are rehearsing their triumphant opera.
The bulbs are stirring in their beds.
And I perceive a whiff of Spring hope in the air.

He waited another seven days, and again he sent forth the dove out of the ark; and the dove came back to him in the evening, and lo, in her mouth a freshly plucked olive leaf; so Noah knew the waters had receded from the earth.

Genesis 8:10-11

If Jesus Came for Coffee

If Jesus came for coffee,
how would I prepare?
Would I put on some makeup
or rush to brush my hair?
Would I dig out the fancy cups
or let him use my favorite mug?
Would I make Him homemade muffins
or vacuum dog hair from the rug?
Would I tell him all my troubles
or just comment on the weather?
Would I remember all my questions
or simply delight we are together?

Perhaps He already comes for coffee
in the morning when I pray.
Remains to hear my lengthy wishes
before I go off about my day
And I don't realize that he listens
because there are no dirty dishes.

Pray without ceasing.

I Thessalonians 5:17

Sunrise Over Shorty's
(March 17, 2022)

Across the highway, sunrise beckons
Indigoes, violets, plums, and peaches
Beyond my sightline on it reaches
More glory now than I can reckon

from my kitchen window distant
blurry sections blocked from view
by gas pumps and a truck or two
A glimpse of heav'n, for an instant.

And so, it is with all our lives
God reveals pieces at a time
so we will not be overwhelmed

by the whole rolled out before our eyes
and how our months and years do rhyme
before we reach the heavenly realm.

A partial sunrise I behold
and watch as ombres morph to gold.

***For now we see in a mirror dimly,
but then face to face.
Now I know in part;
then I shall understand fully,
even as I have been fully understood.***

I Corinthians 13:12

Hero

Hero hadn't lived up to her name.
In fact most days she felt like a bystander
in her own life
while events unfolded much the same
way as they always had.
beyond her control.

She watched from the sidelines
without opposition or consent.
An impartial observer,
while other more knowledgeable
and vocal people made decisions on her behalf
and told her what to think.

She believed in God
but in a distant and impersonal way.
He was to her, a million miles away,
concerned with more important matters
beyond the weather in her tiny town
or the growing crack in her car windshield,
or when to plant her garden this year.

When the scraggly gray kitten appeared
behind the trashcans at work,
she assumed it would either wonder off
or someone else would come to collect it.
When neither happened by the end of the day
(and the kitten meowed at her pitifully)
she felt the strange urge to pick it up.

This puzzled her greatly
because she was not a fan of animals in general,
or of cats, in particular.
Still, she gently lifted it up,
cradled it inside her coat, (because it was a windy day),
and hurried home,

As she nursed the kitten back to health,
felt his warm purr rumble against her chest,
and witnessed how he looked at her
with such open adoration
when she came through the door each afternoon,
something shifted inside her.

She began to see herself through the kitten's eyes.
To him, she was not a spectator
or a tumbleweed in the wind.
She was the Hero.
To him, she was the provider of all good things.
He seemed to know she loved him unequivocally
and loved her completely in return.

And gradually, the idea bloomed in heart,
that perhaps, the God she believed in from afar,
cared not only about the big overwhelming issues;
Wars, pandemics, and politics,
but about small things too,
like the welfare of a stray kitten.

And that, maybe, he cared about her personally
and had given her a part to play
in his grand story.
Her pulse quickened at the thought.

So, while helping with big problems
seemed beyond her reach,
she could actively participate in
the little courageous roles
assigned to her each day.
And in all good time
grow into her name.
Hero.

***And who knows whether you have not come to the kingdom
for such a time as this.***

Esther 4:14b

Snow on Easter

April 17, 2022

Snow? On Easter Sunday?
What a strange sight!
Should glimpse buds of new life celebration
out the window, not downy flakes of white.
Where are gentle winds of Spring elation?

I tire of heavy coats strewn by the door.
Be gone wool hats hiding static tresses.
Bare those arms, and twirl those Easter dresses
Burst forth the bright Spring flowers I adore.

Then, I got to contemplating the white.
How fresh snow blankets the ground anew
How it repaints our muddy April plight
Just like Jesus' love cleanses me and you.

His forgiveness makes souls pure as new snow.
So, sing Hallelujah and let joy flow!

Come now, let us reason together, says the Lord
though your sins are like scarlet,
they shall be as white as snow;
though they are red like crimson,
they shall become like wool.

Isaiah 1:18

Apple Trees
May 2022

Apple saplings planted on our hill
four yellow, two red,
Six willowy trunks swaying in the raucous wind
The birth of an orchard.

The house is not started,
the barn is not finished,
the horses are not yet grazing,
the chickens are not pecking in their pen,
But our gravel road ends with apple trees.

A late Spring,
inflation soaring,
gas prices high,
war in Europe,
political unrest at home,
parents angry at schools,
schools suspecting of parents,
folks wanting more government,
others wanting less,
people wanting more police protection,
others demanding less.
cultural strife
heavy-handed opinions
"We the people" appear fractious, gloomy, and fearful.

Despite all this
my husband and daughter brought home saplings.
We buried root balls in the rich dark soil
Mulched and marked them by fence circles.
A refreshing act of hopefulness
that won't bear fruit for a handful of years.
An investment in our future life
and perhaps someone else's.

What does hope look like you ask?
Hope is trees on hill.
But you already knew that.

"Even if I knew that tomorrow the world would go to pieces, I would still plant my apple tree."

Martin Luther

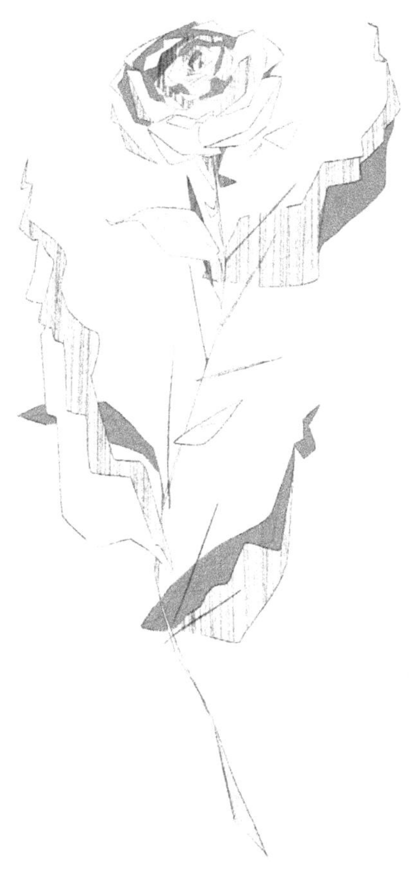

Graduation May 2022

Dear Friend,

There were white roses with sharp thorns.
Isn't that always the way of it?
In the midst of a beautiful celebratory day,
I get pricked by unsettling emotions
that I have to work through
by laying them bare to you.

Allow me to begin before the thoughts in my mind
scatter like so much gold and silver confetti on our carpet

I wish I could share with you some profound wisdom gleaned
from my eldest's high school graduation ceremony.
Tell you how the fourteen bright-eyed seniors garbed in
black or white inspired a tired Gen X mom with hope for the
future of our country,
expound on the importance of ceremonial rites of passage
and neatly encapsulate the lot with a quote.

But I find my feelings regarding the day
more like wiggly leftover Jell-O Salad.
I have trouble congealing them into words
let alone pouring the words into lines wrought with meaning.

First, I must confess,
by the time Saturday afternoon rolled around
I was so strung out from party preparations
that much of the actual graduation was a blur.

These things I remember:
White roses with sharp thorns,
a magic trick, appropriate student speeches with some humor,
not having any idea what I was supposed to do (again), while
everyone else seemed certain,
awareness of people missing,
the surreal feeling that this was all happening to someone
else because I could not possibly be old enough to have a
daughter graduating from high school,
and relief.

Relief that we'd made it to this day after the fear and
isolation of a pandemic
and the physical and emotional turmoil
of moving cross country.
Relief that my daughter had been accepted to a University
Relief that she has jobs
and relief that she smiled a lot and got invited to other parties
with friends.

Another confession.
I didn't cry, which is unusual, isn't it?
When she graduated from the eighth grade at the Charter School,
I wept.
I knew those children from kindergarten.
I had helped in their classrooms,
chaperoned their field trips,
joked with their parents at soccer games and concerts,
and stood in the rain with them at the neighborhood bus stop.

Saturday, as I watched the slide show morph babies
into a row of handsome and elegant graduates,
it was clear that the whole town knew and loved these children in the
same way I loved those eighth graders.

They had followed their elementary school and high school careers
through church, school, and town newspaper.
They had celebrated their successes and mourned their failures,
while we were someplace else
living other lives with other people.

To me, her classmates were practically strangers
or at most, distant acquaintances.
They had painfully lost one of their own along the way
which bonded them tightly in their grief.
So much so, that it blurred the lines between their grief over her and
the joy of their celebration.

Not that anyone was unkind to our girl,
quite the contrary.
She was now an adopted daughter
a grafted vine,
a legacy, other's in my husband's family having graduated from the
same school,
Her photograph will now be with the 2022 Seniors
in the hallway for always.

Overall, the day was a beautiful
with some thorns to keep it real.

The Lord Bless you and keep you:
The Lord make his face to shine upon you,
and be gracious to you;
The Lord lift his countenance
upon you and give you peace.

Numbers 6:24-26

What Storytellers Know

Each character emerges for a purpose.
They have a specific job to do and a reason for existing
They bring unique traits into play
pivotal to particular scene or chapter.

They might shed light on a facet of the main character's personality,
illustrate their humor,
offer comic relief from the intensity of their plight,
be balm in times of grief or hardship,
open a window to their flaws,
illuminate the struggle they are meant to overcome.
relate a crucial piece of information
be a friend or confidant,
relate a backstory,
serve as a predecessor or an ancestor,
act as a sounding board for ideas,
a cheerleader, a messenger, a deliverer, or a planner.

On the flip side, they might offer a contrast to the main character
in the form of a worthy opponent, rival, or enemy,
Someone in need of redeeming grace.
the dark to their light.

Characters are not written in casually.
It is far too much work to imagine their complexities,
name them,
breathe life into their flat images,
design them flawed enough to be relatable
but not so flawed that the audience does not sympathize with some
part of their personality.

Even minor characters shed light on the hero.
And villains illuminate the hero by contrast.
Without a cast or at least some illusion to other characters
there is but endless empty monologue.

So, I'm thinking,
if I, a mere human writer,
put so much thought and effort into
lovingly designing characters for my stories,
imagine what tremendous care and attention to detail,
the Greatest Storyteller of all puts into creating us.

So, the next time I doubt my purpose
or flirt with despair over perceived failures,
I will remember the foreshadowing,
seeming coincidences, and
unexpected friendships.

Play through my backstory
ponder how my griefs, and experiences unlocked empathy
be amazed by the unexpected joys
consider how my small insignificant acts
may have provided pieces for someone else's story.

I'll think about how God
is always putting things in motion,
and setting stage for future events,
that transpire in the fullness of time.

Then, I'll spiral out
to consider how He masterfully orchestrates
billions of simultaneous, interwoven stories
past, present, and future
with such perfect intention.

I don't know all the pieces He's put in motion,
I cannot comprehend why evil
has such sway over current events,
or understand why opposing groups
seem so set on strife.

I *do* know, that I should be fretting less about my failures
and focusing more on my role
in the business of spreading
the Good News,
and reflecting Jesus' light to the world,
one story at a time.

How beautiful on the mountains are the feet of those who bring good news, who proclaim peace, who bring good tidings, who proclaim salvation, who say to Zion "Your God reigns."

Isaiah 52:7

A Night at the Barrel Races

On certain May evenings when the weather is fair
and a gentle Spring breeze toys with tendrils of hair
the rodeo grounds open up for some races.
The kind that put smiles on cowgirls' tan faces.

Horse trailers towed in all sizes and shapes
converge on the grounds and drop tailgates agape.
From their shadowy tunnels emerge their athletes
ready to run, and their courses complete

Sorrels, bright buckskins, roans, dapple grays,
Paints, and palominos glowing gold in late day,
Hues of bay; from penny to near black.
So, many colors it's hard to keep track.

From smallest of ponies to strong geldings and mares
all brushed 'til they shine with braids in their hair.
Donning tooled saddles with their high cantle heights
and elegant bridles with brow bands so bright.

They paw at the earth. With impatience they dance
awaiting their name call and today's perfect chance.
The opening gate, the starting clock tick.
the thump of the heels, and off like a rocket.

They charge toward the first metal barrel with flare.
while on the loud speaker country tunes blare.
Whipping around to the cheers from the stands
Tilted far to one side, knee deep in the sand.

Away to the second, the team sprints on slipping.
So close to the barrel, a hairbreadth from tipping.
It rocks in its place but stays where it's at.
And, they gallop on, rider losing her hat,

Fired like a slingshot around that last barrel
Sailing toward home with ponytails flying
Hooves barely touching, bodies outstretching
To halt at the very last instant, breath catching.

Announcer calls time to the hundredths of seconds
Patted and praised, now the horse's hay beckons
While the next team to run, snorts and prances in place,
ready to burst through the gate for their race.

"...and let us run with perseverance the race that's set before us."

Hebrews 12:1b

Goldfinches

Goldfinches, goldfinches by the bunches
descend for breakfasts, snacks, and lunches
swarm the feeders, seeking seeds
Chirping over winter deeds.

Males painted vivid sunshine yellow
fly here and there with friends and fellows.
Converge on swinging fast food houses.
Overshadowing mellow greenish spouses.

Lighting up those cloudy Spring days
with feathers bright as July rays.
Filled with energy, life and humor
Spreading new hope faster than a rumor.

Did they come from some warm southern clime
to lay their eggs and fuel my rhyme?
Or were they here all winter long?
drab camo birds awaiting joyful songs.

So, when hope sags for a dreary season
and life lacks all brilliant hopeful reason
Hides 'neath snow and wind and freezing rain
or dulls with heartache, grief, or pain

Ponder goldfinches by the vibrant bunches.
and soon you'll be smiling…I have a hunch
Watch their bright feathers dappling greening lawns,
illuminating the bleak and foggy dawn.

.

Now hope that is seen is not hope.
For who hopes for what he sees?
But if we hope for what we do not see,
we wait for it with patience.

Romans 8:24-25

Memorial Day

If now you are feeling somehow slighted
by our highly vocal fractious nation.
Begin to think all politics blighted
and worry over children's education.

If patriotic fire has died to embers
along with faith in founding fathers.
Both parties of Congress members
viewing freedoms as inconvenient bothers.

If red and white stripes for colonies thirteen
with state stars dotting corner field of blue,
seem just a decoration to be seen
and not symbols; courageous, pure and true.

Then, turn off your despairing news feed
for an hour, remove your cynical frowns
and head to Memorial Day on Main Steet
in your own community or town.

Pray the Invocation at the start
sing songs, repeat the Pledge of Allegiance
standing straight and tall with hand over heart
and thank veterans with due diligence.

Listen hard to the Roll Call of the Dead,
Soldiers lost in many different wars
left their homes and fam'lies to serve instead
Fighting for freedoms too precious to ignore.

A long list of names filled with untold tales
of our brave soldiers and heroic acts
of far-off battles and lengthy sails
of jungles, trenches and friendship pacts.

So, next time you're angry at red or blue
Thank God for our freedom to disagree.
Recall all we, *united* have been through
and those who fought with faith to keep us free.

**But we are not those who shrink back and are destroyed
but of those who have faith and keep their souls.**

Hebrews 10:39

The Horses Are Home
May 2022

Knee deep in thick grass so green,
it looks almost blue,
our horses, Gypsy and Cherry,
the shining bay and the golden buckskin,
grazing in the pasture on own piece of prairie.
The wind blowing their long manes
and the grass rippling in waves
breaking gently against their legs.
A backdrop of soft azure sky
complete with white puffy
clouds on the perfect late spring day.
Cattle dotting the hillside.

I know now that we were sojourners in suburbia.
Yes, it's been harder than we thought
and there has been a steep learning curve
We still don't have a house built
and probably won't for at least another year.
But there is a red barn on the hill
and a couple horses
and the apple saplings.

Praise God from whom all blessings flow.

Doxology

Pansies

Painted petals dance.

A purple pansy party,

playing on our porch

Bean Sprouts

Bean sprouts popping up,

breathing early summer blue,

bending in the breeze.

Dandelions

Dandelions sneeze.

Spreading their golden germs with

Silent snowy roars.

Sunset

Bright swirling shades.

A Shirley Temple sunset.

Oh, to drink the sky.

Holy Spark

Why waste your holy spark on such as me?
Far too spent and squishy in the tummy,
an impatient, graying mother of three.
Frumpy, and with failure far too chummy.
You, who filled the vast cobalt rolling sea,
freed your people from the shade of mummy
calmed roaring wind, and bled upon the tree
to clean our souls so foul and scummy.

Still, you breathe fire into my humble veins
to paint with words and weave light-filled stories
of fragrant flowers and singing sparrows.
of purring kittens and dark flowing manes
of epic loving and dragon glories
of amber marigolds and wild yarrow.

When I look at the heavens, the work of thy fingers,
the moon and stars which though hast established;
What is man that thou are mindful of him,
and the son of man that thou dost care for him?

Psalm 8: 3-4

Wild Phlox

If I had hair like that wild phlox
unveiled behind newly cut rye,
If from my head grew violet locks,
I'd never consent them to dye,

Nor to cut the tresses the wind
makes dance 'neath a cloudless June sky.
Nor in a cap hide hair pinned
where it wilts and begins to die.

I would relish blooms unbound
hanging heavy to my waist.
A lacy sundress as a gown
with no fragile petal a waste.

No graying roots brushed tight in a tail.
Just the glory of summer unveiled.

***The flowers appear on the earth,
the time of singing has come.***

Song of Solomon 2:11

Belonging

Move enough times and you learn
that belonging is elusive.
Always just outside one's grasp
A hairbreadth beyond that line in the sand.

You're either too young or too old
Too dark or too light
Too short or too tall
Too plump or too slender
Too salty or too bland
Too sweet or too spicy
Too novice to be accepted
Too seasoned to be cutting edge
Too blue to be red
Too red to be blue

Not the life of the party
Not quite a hermit.
Not popular enough to be "In"
Not fringe enough to be cool.

But if you look closely
Most people defy categories,
They are abstract distillations of their experiences
not contained by an artificial box drawn by another.
We are all sojourners in this world
awaiting true belonging in the next.

So, then you are no longer strangers and sojourners,
but you are fellow citizens with the saints, and members of
the household of God.

Ephesians 2:19

On Rejection

A curt rejection email
after a patriotic holiday weekend
causes past refusals to rise like bile
in the back of my throat.
A casual dismissal of my whole precious manuscript.
Poisoned barbed words strike
hopelessness and failure into my soul.
I feel betrayed, belittled, angry, insecure
itching to defend myself.
My dander is up.
The enemy smiles.
This is his deceitful attempt to shake me.

I cry out to God
and text a Prayer Warrior.
Receive a knowing embrace from my husband
Stew while making supper.
Go to practice and sing my heart out.
Boiling anger recedes to simmering tears.
By the next day, I am able to reply politely-
deleting all passive aggressive words.

Remember, God loves me.
He put poems and stories in my heart.
He is orchestrating some other plan of which I know not.
I must endure the rejections, the brush offs, the ghosting.
I will persevere.
I will shun bitterness.
I will remain faithful.
I will not stoop to writing trash
or respond to meanness with unkindness.

With the Lord on my side, I do not fear. What can man do to me?
The Lord is on my side to help me; I shall look in triumph on those
who hate me.

Psalm 118:6-8

Battling Weeds

Every tiller of soil battles weeds.
They pop up after the rain and if left unchecked
take root and flourish into bushes
choking the life out of the good plants and grasses.
They take-over, blocking the sunlight
until all that was fresh and fruitful
vanishes in shadow and we forget
what seed was planted in the first place.

These days we are choked by the weeds of bad news.
Even when not actively searching,
headlines pop up while emailing a friend,
or viewing a how-to video,
or checking the weather,
distracting us from our mission.
They shadow our thoughts with
fear, anger and anxiety.

Bad news weeds like
High gas prices.
Soaring inflation
A border in crisis
War in Europe.
Abortion divisions
Political mudslinging
And Covid ever lingering in the background
These weeds and others,
take root in our hearts,
threatening those we hold dear and
stealing our hope.

Only faith keeps these weeds from blocking true Sonlight.
We must re-focus on The Good News
Remember God sent his son to save us.
Cultivate fruits of the spirit
so instead of weeds, we can witness flowers blooming,
zucchini nubs on the vine,

green tomatoes,
blossoms on the peas and beans
fields of alfalfa
and thigh-high corn

Yes, our hands will get dirty weeding
and our muscles ache,
but in the end,
the labor will be worthwhile
and bear good fruit.

For no good tree bears bad fruit, nor again does a bad tree bear good fruit; for each tree is known by its own fruit. For figs are not gathered from thorns, nor are grapes picked from a bramble bush.

Luke 6: 43-44

Zinnias
July

Spring droplets of rain on flower seeds glean
a mid-summer radiant paint pallet.
From pale yellow hues and soft tangerine
to pumpkin pie, magenta, and scarlet.

Bright colors splash in a leafy green sea.
Joined roots linked arm in arm against breezes.
Not shoving, fighting, or speaking off-key.
A lovingly face-tinted parade crowd.

A thought occurs, as I text pics to Mother.
Shouldn't people be more like zinnias?
Valued, unique, but still standing together
and loving their neighbors like family.

One zinnia got no note or comment.
The unified bed inspired a sonnet.

**Behold how good and pleasant it is
when brothers dwell in unity!**

Psalm 133:1

Off to College

August

Yesterday you were the baby
who emerged red-faced and screaming
into my shaking, untrained arms.

Today you are a bold, lovely, complicated woman
embracing the future with clear-eyed intention
and dramatic style.

There is no stoic way to say good-bye.
Only hugs and well-wishes
last minute advice
secret prayers
a final kiss thrown from the skyway
and a long solitary drive home
through fields primed for harvest
with red eyes and damp cheeks.

The Lord will keep you from all evil; he will keep your life. The Lord will keep your going out and your coming in from this time forth and forever more.

Psalm 121:7-8

Tomatoes

"A poem about tomatoes?"
asked the skeptic walking by
But I'm grateful for our harvest
so I'll give this rhyme a try.

We never had tomatoes like
the plethora this year.
Every time I spy my kitchen counter,
I feel like God deserves a cheer.

Usually, they crack or wilt
or get eaten up by pests.
Too much water or not enough?
I never seem to know what's best.

But this year they are perfect
and that's a documented fact.

Bright red plums and ruby cherries
on a tangled mass of vines
Don't get me started on the yellows
in huge globes of gold sunshine.

To family and friends,
I've given away bunches
Had them sliced for supper
and every day for lunches.

I made salsa, three kinds so far
dehydrated halved cherries
and canned fresh pasta sauce in jars.

But today when I was mowing
(and watching out for snakes)
I saw more ripe for picking,
and thought 'for goodness sakes!'

She prepares her food in summer, and gathers sustenance in harvest. Proverbs 6:8

Green Pastures

*G*reen pastures spell
*R*elief to those caring for livestock.
*E*ndless summer days with
*E*ver full bellies and
*N*o panic to buy hay bales.

*P*raying that you
*A*lways have the comfort
*S*pace and freedom embodied by green pastures.
*T*hat you will flourish
*U*nder the Good Shepherd's care and guidance
*R*esting in His arms
*E*ating at His table and
*S*preading His love until we meet again.

The Lord is my shepherd, I shall not want. he makes me lie down in green pastures. He leads me beside still waters; he restores my soul. He leads me in the paths of righteous for his name's sake.

Psalm 23: 1-3

Acknowledgements

First and foremost, thank you to the Holy Spirit for the creative inspiration and ideas. A special thank you to my daughter, Noelle for the spectacular illustrations and cover art. Thank you to my daughter Holly, for listening with a gentle ear to first versions of many of the poems. Thank you to my husband, Lynn for his patience and technical help. Thank you to my family and close friends for reading the poems I sporadically emailed out and replying with good humor and encouragement. It is appreciated more than you will ever know.

Works Cited

The New Oxford Annotated Bible with Apocrypha.

   Edited by Herbert G. May and Bruce M. Metzger, Oxford University Press 1977.

The Christian Doxology. Anglican Bishop Thomas Ken.